a pocket of love, dark poetry, and prose

mckenzie vlad

BookLeaf
Publishing

India | USA | UK

Presentation by *BookLeaf Publishing*

Web: www.bookleafpub.com

E-mail: info@bookleafpub.com

ISBN: 9789363311299

First edition 2024

contents

epigraph

the moon is also alone;
but still, it shines the brightest
even when it's not perfectly round.

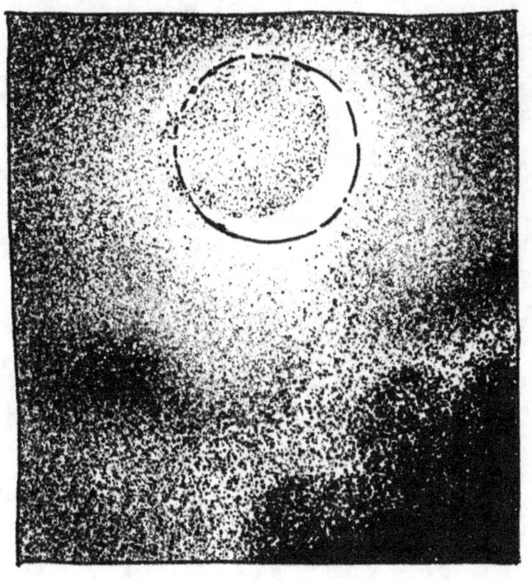

i hope you feel whole on days
when you feel as if you aren't enough
or when things seem out of place.

*∞ please know that you are
and will always be enough ∞*

an unrequited love

in the calmness i possess, there's stillness
that lingers in silence with a faint hope,
seeking in vain for clues to brew relentlessly—
like the sound of coffee brewing that deafens
to the ears and makes my blood run cold.

each night, when i lie in the dark,
i embark on a journey to escape this gritty reality,
waiting patiently for your warm embrace.

i, however, lose you again and again
when the awakening comes to life
with a blinding light that seemingly
appears like a blazing sun.

then as i reach for your hand to hold
these fragments of my vivid imagination,
your lips have parted in a smile,
splitting my heart into two.

maybe it's just me secretly pondering
on an aura of mystery, pinning my hopes
on this whole fantasy of unrequited love;
cursed to curb like an ecstasy drug.

maybe you know, judging by my fiery blush
as a hot summer of excitement, hesitance,
and so much giggling when you're around;
or maybe you don't and we'll never be upfront
about it, to spit it out without fear of rejection
and disappointment.

i hope there comes a day when we both part ways,
our hair turns gray, our teeth decay to raggedness;
that'll be the day for me to array my bewildering
complexity of an emotionless mask;
that's how i knew the tragedy of unrequited love.

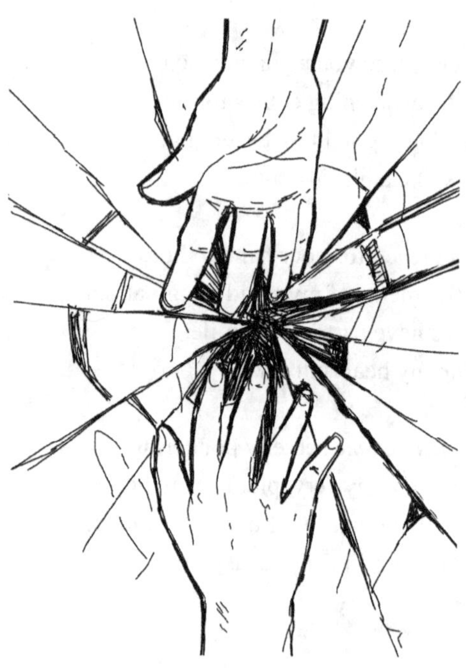

25

life consists of different pieces
that are meant to be well-assembled
and put together: one whole jigsaw puzzle.

on one hand, it's a paradox composed
of fascinating stories, fulfillments, and obstacles.

on the other, it's a riddle of open-ended questions
and what-ifs; but quite often, they fall in between.

when we look at life without rose-colored glasses,
we'll begin to think with sinking thoughts that…

perhaps, life is full of questions that remain
up in the air in all respects; ironically,
we hold our keys to those sealed caskets.

perhaps, life is full of choices
we tend to dwell upon—
we can choose to hold on to pain
and gain nothing but anguish,
or we can choose to let it slide
and succumb to temptation.

like the sea that ebbs and flows over time,
everything will fall into place
when we embrace change to thrive.

so, when you look at life as you turn 25,
you'll understand why life prepares you
to defy gravity and set you free
from a spanner in the works.

what love is

love is gracious and solicitous
without the need to say *i love you*
to show affinity—

like a couple sitting at a dinner table,
smiling, having fun; pondering about
what to begin?
what to say?
what to ask?

or, candidly put,
what would you like to eat?
how was your day?

love is feeling enough without affirmation—
like a queer person unapologetically being themself;
you can see it through the way they dress,
the way they talk, the way they behave.
they love themself enough
never to question if they are enough.

love is consolation and fellow feeling—
like a stranger helping a homeless person
seek shelter from the rain, or offering them
a place for the night.

and it doesn't matter if it's just a makeshift one,
for love is needed in a state of emergency.

m'pay bay village

on a late saturday afternoon, when the moon soon
appeared in the clear-blue sky cast by the pale light
of a halo that was oh-so-beautifully-rounded,
i caught a plain sight of its glimmer disguised by
white patches of clouds, passing unnoticed as if
they were dancing gleefully with the wind.

however cozy the moon glowed, it was no better
than how blinding the sun shone in its golden hour,
glowing red with the heat yet gentle and warm to
my sun-kissed cheeks as it was descending gracefully
from the west, blessing the whole village and all
living things on the sandy m'pay bay of the tropical
koh rong sanloem with the gleam of the setting sun
and a renewed hope of what's to come tomorrow.

while the sun was sinking below the horizon,
glinting off the distant mountains,
the moon remained lucent in the firmament
until the sun disappeared from view
and the moonlight began anew.

i savored the moment in that instant,
astonished by how the sun and the moon
turned to each other for solace as
a perfect yin and yang as two halves that beat as

one—the likes of which i hadn't seemed to notice
before.

perhaps, the way the moon gives strength to the sun
is to teach us that love is more than a display of
affection—*love is the essence of devotion and
patience.*

my gentleness

i grew up thinking that there must have been
something wrong with my gentleness and quietness,
or how i wore my solemn expression
which somehow was considered intimidating to
hostile kids: the bullies.

perhaps, that's just the way they thought—
all in their heads like a buzzing fly
that got inside their ears, zizzing furiously.
it never found a way out.

perhaps, it caused or triggered such unease in their
stomachs. a thunderous sound, i suppose.
but they never came to understand their starvation,
their thirst for grace; deprived of the food of courtesy.

perhaps, i didn't feel the need to fight back or intend
to, like cats and dogs; for fighting never ends or
resolves, yet it turns into nothing but remorse and
animosity.

ever heard of a series of unfortunate events?
that seems a lot like it, or it can possibly be worse.
a chain that never ends is a chain of conflicts.

to not be engaged in a fight is to stay aloof from the
bickering. one must put up a wall of defense to avoid
being flooded by unnecessary rage and temperament.

ill will is pointless, and so not wise.
be kinder by all means.

letting go

sometimes, staying hurts more than leaving.
so, if you've decided to remove yourself from a
situation that has filled you with self-doubt,
apprehension, and unworthiness, know that
i'm so very proud of you.

it's going to hurt, but you'll make it through—
and, darling, one day you'll look back
and thank yourself for pulling through.

cry if you want to, for grief is a natural response to
loss. loneliness will be there, but try to think of it as
nightmares because they don't last. things like this
take time, so try not to blame yourself for what
happened.

seasons change. even flowers bloom and die.
nothing lasts forever. remember that pain,
whether emotional or physical, is temporary.
you matter, and you are whole.

i hope you are proud of who you are
and whatever you've overcome.

choose what makes you happy
and what feels right to you.

you are wonderfully you.
never forget that.

kindness

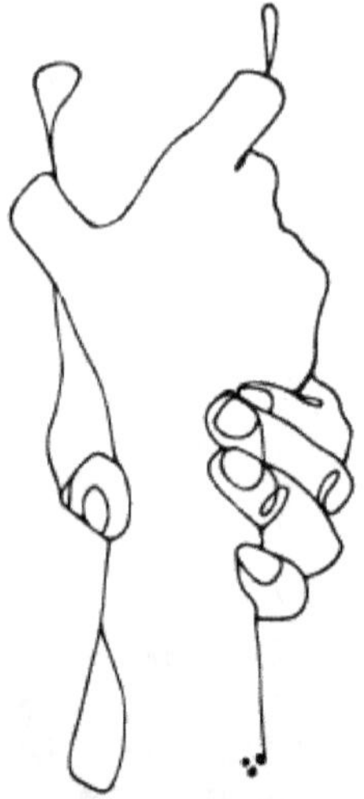

kindness comes from your best intentions—
and your donations, *however small,*
can offer those in need homely shelters
and sheltered lives.

a used blanket keeps a homeless person
(or even a family) tucked safely and warmly at night,
especially when the rain falls and the lights go out—
for the only thing left is that brisk and gusty wind,
chilling to the bone.

some say money is the key to happiness,
as it gives us access to most things in life.

giving breeds transports of delight
that guide us to seventh heaven
while our feet are still on the ground,
building an air of elegance around us.

the more we give, the more we receive in return—
that kind of unconditional love that warms the
cockles of someone's heart and feeds our souls.

offer today, as tomorrow might never come.

heartbreak

a heartbreak aches like nothing else—
it tears you limb from limb: a shredding mess.

feelings fade, though haunting memories remain,
lingering still like an irrevocable step you can't take
back.

as the saying goes, *absence makes the heart grow
fonder* (come to think of it, *does it really concur in
reality?*)

rather, i've seen absence bring nothing but bitterness
held dear by those who love with all their heart.

grin and bear it; if you shift your focus onto your lot
in life with meticulous attention,
you'll find out why one thing
is attached to another: nothing appears intact.

so, my friend, the next time you have your heart
broken, gently remind yourself to take a deep breath,
have a little faith, and give yourself time to heal:
healing is a process.

…and when you're ready to rise again,
be sure to fly high like a bird set free.

i do hope you fall in love with someone
who would never wish to break your heart.

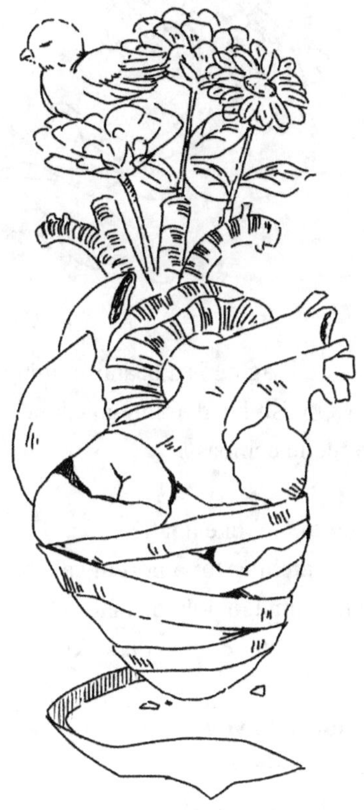

aging

not entirely sure if aging is a beautiful thing.
there are days i wish i had a time-machine
and/or a magnetic compass.

i'm beginning to feel like a tattered,
bustling ship searching for a port of call.
the stars seem unimaginably distant
but usually come into view in dark skies.

each star belongs to you
if you let it cloud over
and light up the sky above.

it's sweet knowing i've made it this far
but kind of gut-wrenching in a way knowing
lost time can't be recouped, bought,
or made up for; my dad told me the other day,
that's how we grow old, unwittingly we get fragile,

some die of unknown fate, our life is a compass of
ambiguities—full of misery to some, even;
we can't hazard a guess, hence we each learn to swim
through dirt and rocks towards the shore.

grief

grief knocks the stuffing
out of me like tidal waves
crashing on the shore relentlessly—
they come rushing in, lugging ripples
of vehemence and havoc galore.

each wave seeks to occlude my very breath,
suffocating my soul's eupnea. my transparency
with grief leaves me on pins and needles,
lost in the depths of dyspnea.

to be left with grief, inconsolable,
a weight that pulls on my weary heart.
i've ridden the surf of it, but each time
i fall, i drown in the sea of despair, torn apart.

the waves loom high above,
their power overwhelming,
a tempest in my mind.
i'm tossed and turned,
unable to find solid ground,
no respite can i find.

a wedding frame

you look happier in a wedding frame
with someone who archly makes you smile
from ear to ear.

i shouldn't be jealous,
i should've known better,
i should be over you by now.

it's been years since you disappeared
from view—out of sight, out of mind.

but, somehow, i still remember
that starless night when we said goodbye
and the moon hung low in the sky.

i knew all too well that the universe
wouldn't bestow any plans for us,
but falling for you was an unsolicited gaffe.

i know it's ludicrous for me to keep blaming
the universe for giving you the nod to cross over
that river into my bridle path, but life oftentimes
is just an unreliable company already.

a bird with clipped wings

it's not funny how you treated me. you let me fall for you so that you could leave me unwanted and tormented. if i could paint an image from that lesion, it would be a picture of a bird with clipped wings still stuck inside an open cage.

did you expect me to just fly away as you wished me to while i was covered in blood? i wish there were a word more intense than 'loathing' to describe how i'm feeling towards you now. i wonder if you ever paused for a second to ponder what you had done, the damage you had inflicted.

you led me on like a fucking fool or a clown that put
on the most ridiculous circus show exclusively for
you. *had you planned the fire to ignite and petrify so
that you could make a mess of it or watch me burn
for it left you cold? how dare you say that i pushed
you away after i'd written a sweet-sounding poem for
you as a way to convey my pure affections and
intentions?*

you said that you didn't want to hurt me after you'd
gnawed at my flesh and poured salt on it.

i guess it was just easy for you to put it that way
because you weren't the one thrust onto a chopping
board like a fish from your diverting pool to be
slashed, peeled, and lacerated just for fun. perhaps i
was just one of the most unfortunate to have fallen
for your deceptive baits.

i should have trusted my gut before you gutted me
without any mercy.

i can see it clearly now that you were trouble from
the start when you started making me wait for 9 hours
or more just for your single-line text of apology. *were
you busy screwing around? were you busy
committing more crimes of infidelity? were you busy
beating around the bush to make someone else fall
under your grasp as another victim? were you busy
planting more love bombs? were you busy putting on*

*other circus shows so that you could send in your
favorite clowns to penetrate you?*

never mind, though. i got all the answers i needed. i
wasn't yours to keep, and you weren't even mine to
cherish. we were just a moment, right? as you
proudly proclaimed. i wish i hadn't known your
existence. i had been a lot happier before you
bantered me with those sex-crazed talks, and i was
too credulous to take them as gospel, coaxed into
your charms—foolish me, thinking that i was
significant to you.

i keep asking the universe why they allowed you to
come into my life to ruin my life party, me, my hope,
and the idea of you. i don't even regret it. i'm just
sick and tired of disappointments, and now you're
one of them.

a permission

this is your permission
to feel all the feels to grieve,
to laugh, or to just cry;
there's no denying
that this life will try
to defy you at times,
even at your lowest points.

they said that grief comes in waves
so that you may learn how to ride the surf
while enjoying the ride...
even though it may be hard at first.

the fear and joy of living
can co-exist at once.
i may not be able to
imagine your pain
or what you're going through,
but i can assure you
that time will take the edge off
your burdens, one by one.

give it time and see how
the road to recovery looks like.
allow yourself to be gravity
that pulls through highs
and lows of emotions,
beckoning you to follow suit.

a guy with ocean eyes

i met a guy with ocean eyes
on a wild night out at a crowded bar,
filled with laughter, cheer,
and contemporary beats to die for.

i was starstruck, caught in the heat of the moment,
when we were introduced. awkwardly for me,
because... *damn, what a sight for sore eyes!*

that memory, still here,
dancing joyfully in my head.
*is it all right to just admit that it had been forever
since my heartskipped a beat?*

when i first saw him,
my heart went untamed,
enraptured by his crooked smile
and husky voice.

putting chemistry to the test
has never been my interest
as it may seem fiddly at times.

but in that instant,
all i knew was,
i was enchanted to meet him.

then i learned he was taken,
another already claimed his heart.

a bittersweet revelation,
a sting beneath the spark.

but even with the knowledge
that he belongs to another's dreams,
i cherish the moment we shared,
however fleeting it seems.

for in that brief encounter,
he left a mark on me,
a reminder of beauty,
in the vast, wild sea.

happier

saw you walking down the street
in a town that never sleeps with
your new boyfriend, but when i said *hi,*
you turned around and a trace of smile
played across your lips; it looked just like
a kid that had just sipped his favorite vanilla
milkshake—simply sweet with a bitter aftertaste
for a story that was never burgeoned into
what we'd painted and pictured as happily ever after.

i still remember how we used to lay entwined
in each other's arms, alarmed by our past stories
that had ceased with a bloody war and a permanent
scar, but we'd rather not talk about it.
what if we had? still springs to mind at times
when your favorite songs shuffle into my playlist
and hot flashes of the sun tickle my skin.

you're now awake in someone else's arms,
laughing heartily at his still jokes,
happier than ever in disbelief.

they often say that time is of the essence
when we're actually elated; that's what i'd like to
imagine anyway.

still do

it's funny how i still miss you
and think of you even now
without any remorse or guilt.
the universe might have only
vouchsafed us a short time,
but please know that i had
a wonderful time learning
your deep-dark secrets
and fears by heart.

you had me laughing
at your witless jokes
without trying so that
in a moment i felt as if

well, this is it—
we are meant for each other,
though fate got in the way
to blow a hole in our avalon
with a shocking twist.

of course, you're still my favorite crime scene,
and i'm elated to be a victim of the crime
we both committed.

i would lie, but i wouldn't
that i still feel the blood coursing through
my veins at the thought of you smoking
and holding my hand.

is it wrong of me to just ask for more
than what's written in the stars?

the universe has let me down so many times
that i almost gave up hope in the art of gravity.

it's grim to fathom that kind of love
that only has a place in films that warm the cockles
of my heart, because reality oftentimes ends in
tragedy when we anticipate hope as dope.

a beautiful stranger

o beautiful stranger,
you sat there alone, listening to music—
it must have been your favorite,
as it prompted a rush of adrenaline
vividly shown in your wildly erratic performance—
a style of dance for joy, making you sway
unsteadily from side to side,
as though you were put in the spotlight.

no one but i was enchanted to witness
a magnificent and intelligent creature,

having quality time to himself,
while his fingers were flicking through
pages of a book, running along
each letter or word: lost in his world.

o beautiful stranger,
i caught you looking at me at times
for an instant when i cast my eyes
in your direction and met yours.

my heart could not skip a beat,
i swear—*once bitten, twice shy.*

though, could we call it fate,
or shall i call it another heartache
…as you stepped out of the door
without looking back?

i wish you did. really, i still do.
'til then, i realized that fate may create
that sensation of hope, but oftentimes
it can never grant you a hankering.

stalking

after years of stalking you online
like a spy for the fbi
you finally emerged in this cafe,
sitting opposite me at different tables
divided by an imaginary wall—
i wish i could grasp your attention
with just one glance.

you looked so nice like your profile picture
and those damn hot reels. the way you pushed
your hair back shuddered me with such fervor,
driving me insane; *is sanity a sacred thing, though?*
perhaps not. your voice alone should be it.

i'd cherish that with my whole damn heart.
and, damn, you looked so tanned like a brand new
skin,
drawing me in with such scrutiny.

are you the evidence of such perfection
that a man could be, or is it purely a misery
for me to only watch you from afar with
a sinking feeling that you'll never be mine?

a broken glass

as i fixed my gaze on a broken glass
that shattered into little shards,
flying in all directions—
its remnants, fragments, particles,
there, laid on the floor, waiting to be repaired.
could we fix it? (how could we not?)

and the more i observed,
the more intrigued i was,
swiftly at the speed of light;
then, i reflected on life
about how i've clung to life
with abiding faith.

see, this broken glass is more than
what meets the eye. it represents
the chaos we face, the pain we can't deny,
but through shattered pieces,
hope starts to rise, a glimpse of our strength,
hidden behind disguise.

in each shard, a story lies,
waiting to be heard, a tale of resilience,
a song too often blurred,
for we are the menders,
the healers, the ones who restore.

with love and compassion,
we open new doors.
we hold these fragments tight,
with hands full of care,
knowing that in the mending,
we find strength to bear,
the weight of our struggles,
the scars that may remain.

but it's through these cracks,
where beauty finds its reign.

stolen glances

it's alluring how our eyes
can serve as indications
of something more than
physical touch.

there are secrets and explicit
deets exchanged with just stolen glances,
which then form into smiley faces
or question marks, *even*, perceptibly shown
in such ways that flare up.

there was a suggestion of a smile on your lips
as you set your eyes on me with a gleam.

did you do that on purpose,
or was it all an illusion?
i hope it was the former.
was it still a matter of false hope
or delusion if the reason behind that
potently acted as non-verbal communication,
sending a clear signal that you felt it, too?

passion

listen to the sound of passion,
buzzing, flickering within,
engrossing you in aliveness—
like a gift of free will
to keep you so hardcore.

passion brings determination to life;
a vivid sight to behold, to mold,
and to sow the seeds of true purpose.

on one hand, passion is a combination
of love and magnificence;
because along with devotion,
comes a need for perfection.

on the other, passion is the creation
of hope uniquely magnified
like the sky full of dreams—
so alive, so fly, and dynamite—
invisible to the eyes,
though lies beneath the soul.

i picture passion as though
it were a magic wand;
with just a swish and flick of it,
it opens up a portal to a whole new world

filled with imagination and inspiration,
bringing light to life with an abiding faith.

but, above all else, passion is the magic within
that depicts all possibilities one can bring out
without going out of style.

true beauty

there's such beauty
manifested in all aspects of life
if one cares enough to see through
curtains of purity behind a veil of secrecy.

do we even give a damn anymore
about one's innermost stance
that underlies beneath their semblance?
(tell me, can we really see the essence of it?)

true beauty exists within—
it doesn't wear off like the smell of perfume,
yet is prevalent in one's humbleness,
kindness, and understanding.

wouldn't it be irie if we could behold
one's true inner merit with the naked eye?

world at stake

have you ever heard the sound of a gun firing?
first, it comes with a blast—loud enough to wake the
dead, and it kills when a bullet hits the right spot.

anything that comes with a shock wave to scare us
off. *a bad omen*, they said. car sirens, aircraft carriers,
explosions, warning signs prior to emergencies. we
are accustomed to casualties brought upon by such
alarms
that we have failed to gird our loins for something
that lurks and jumps quickly in shadows,
undermining our strength and keeping our cells
at bay.

outbreaks take us by the throat and infuse fear within.
each one launches threats of hellfire, burning on earth
with passion. the burning sensation has left us gagged
with deprivations, which makes us question where
else we could go.

while there's only one planet as a sheltered spot for
sheltered lives, albeit gravely affected,
in danger of falling apart.

shops closed. bars and pubs shut down. schools
postponed. concerts canceled. the only thing that

withers in the wind now is the unusual quietness that
has left nothing but a state of bewilderment,
sending a spiral shiver down everyone's spine.

facts may hurt and may be uncared for, but reality can
be the death of us. it has slaughtered almost every
part that lives, breathes, and walks on earth.

human disruptions are unstoppable, and natural
disasters are the evidence in the aftermath.

this home we all proudly call earth deserves so much
better than how poorly it has been treated as if it were
something to be taken for granted.

fear of the unknown

it was very dark and stark this morning.
it must've been the weather after heavy rainfall the
night before, or me unconsciously waking up in the
middle of the night at 2 to catch the latest news of a
sudden lockdown. *it was wild*—angry comments and
emojis kept popping up like bubbles. some supported
it, some were definitely against it.

i watched that livestream with my eyes wide open
and a heavy heart, fully aware of this unforeseen
nightmare in a ghastly manner, or what's been said
before that the worst is yet to come.

images from what had happened on the preceding
evening still filled me with such terror and trauma.
haunting images like—a flock of people with
brooding and anxious expressions, storming into this

mini-mart nearby (that isn't usually crammed on tuesdays, but was stuffed to the gills on that particular tuesday evening, 15th april 2021) with their baggy bags or backpacks as fat as suitcases, ready to stock as many items as they could grab from the shelves—eggs, snacks, bread, canned foods…you name it.

some looked stunned, wandering through the aisles, hoping to find mighty supplies that would keep their lives afloat. they must've been overly overwhelmed by what's happening, what's really going on; i was so sure of it.

i, too, was engulfed by agitation and my own wretched mind, watching a sea of strangers and some familiar faces walk past, seemingly unaware of the buzz of shopping carts being wheeled—pushed and pulled, back and forth—scratching the floor; the buzz of overflowing conversations, echoing every corner of this place where we could pin our hopes on; or the buzz of wailing toddlers, clutching their small hands with wonder or fear of the unknown.

musings

i've been thinking about...

how pleased the rain gets
to meet and greet the land
whenever the wet season
comes around.

how sparkling the dance floor
becomes when a mirror ball
moves and glistens.

how plants come into flowers
when water and sunlight
are fine and dandy towards the soil.

how the ocean never stops kissing the shoreline.
how the moon rises just as the sun sets
as two halves that beat as one.

how a smile of delight lights up a pet's face
as their owner returns home after a long day at work.

the captain of a senile ship

for such a long time,
i've been the captain
of this senile ship
bound for nowhere,
or no fucking where?

how am i supposed to know
while the ghost of you
is still biding here,
besieging every corner
like a dead town
that never dies.
only dust hangs in the air,
not to mention these musty
and acrid smells.

i was once told that
death isn't an end—
their soul will linger
like an outbreak of plague;
it'll be let out to haunt
and zap the living
with such bitter,
lasting memories…
until their time also calls
for a final exit.

an exit and end

i never saw it coming. a train was speeding towards
me, it jolted into motion with a deafening crash. a
part of me was still clinging to hope that you'd never
leave me like others who had walked in and out of
my life as if it were a loose door without locks.

but somehow you did. you found a way out and
exited without even saying goodbye, as if nothing
had happened between us, as if i were a misery inside
your trapped doors, as if i were just a figment of your
imagination. but, the worst scenario was you
pretending as if i didn't even exist, as if i was already
gone, laying hopelessly still in a graveyard you dug
for me, buried with nothing but remaining memories
scattered like skeletons and ashes.

i sent you a long letter that night at 2 while my eyes
welled up with tears running down my cheeks,
hoping that you would understand when i said, *i'm a
wrecked ship with the lights on underneath the
ocean*—which is to say, i'm a difficult person to love,
but i know how to love you because these lights are
the evidence of my beating heart. but nothing was
returned, not even a damn given.

just seen and gone, you were gone; and i had to come
to terms with the death of you in my life while the

heartbreak was present with such disappointment. i
wasn't even sure of what had led to this
let-down—either you, myself, or this dreadful fate
that made it happen and ended it with a cruel twist.

*but who was i to demand such affection from a
person with conflicted thoughts and confused
feelings?* in the back of my mind, though, i still
wonder if that letter was just an abbreviated piece of
nothing, for you left it there like a dying bird left out
in the cold.

adrift in darkness

i keep running, running,
and running away, off track,
going round in circles, adrift;
as if i wafted through the air,
though feet still on land, without guise,
lacking in direction.

small as an ant, light as a feather,
i waver in the draught;
a hankering for an escape,
a portal to all in fine fettle;
no woe or dolor: hell on earth,
in extremity.

perplexity is a misery inside trapped doors
where i could not see or capture light,
but darkness—it lies there,
with my eyes wide shut.

tidal waves

50

if we aim too high to fly,
we might fall with a broken neck.
these tidal waves never waver,
even when we know better than
to mess with tides that rise above
our might and crash headlong
down the sea.

*see? we quiver when we're touched
to the bone*, letting out a moan
of pleasure or despair,
rarely unnoticed
if we're quick enough
to succumb to pain felt
by no other.

secret encoded love languages

sending love notes to each other.
having a long, cozy chat with open hearts.
would you like to go see this movie?
i know you've been super excited about it.
i wrote a poem for you. here's a cup of your
favorite tea and some cookies to keep you
warm in this weather. would you like to go
outside and grab coffee today?
noticing a friend affected by seasonal depression
and saving a seat for an introverted friend
at a crowded party. giving a homeless person a hug,
some food, and money too, if needed.
sitting with a friend in silence while they cry.
oh, i've already ordered your favorites,
with a reassuring smile.

a thing called love

i believe in a thing called love.
you may not see it,
but you can always feel it.
love exists within.
it follows you everywhere,
no matter where you go,
just like the moon follows the sun,
no matter what else pans out.

your heart opens when you feel
and receive love all around.
yet, it's also important to
shower yourself with
lots of tender loving care.

self-love is neither selfish
nor egocentric—it's the act
of cradling your well-being with care,
especially when you're plunged into
a total eclipse of the heart.

departure

in the sleepless hours before my departure,
i found myself amidst a journey's overture.
scenes of excitement and lamentation
filled the air, love, laughter, and tears
intertwined rare.

walking past one terminal to another,
i stumbled through a sea of strangers,
tangled by emotions—hugging, kissing,
weeping, or waiting for someone to show.

an airport gate, a portal to worlds unknown,
could make you leap for joy when you're homesick;
yet it could also pull you down in the dumps,
as the gate closes, separation happens
like heart-wrenching thumps.

the echoes of longing reverberate through the halls,
whispers of souls singing bittersweet calls.
strangers' stories intermingling,
like a tapestry divine, each carrying hopes,
dreams, and cherished moments left behind.

but amidst this tumultuous symphony,
there's a flame of resilience that burns fiercely.
for airports are not just places of departure and
arrival, they are catalysts for connections,
both fleeting and vital.

in those fleeting moments, lives intertwine,
and for a breath, we become part of each other's
design—sharing smiles, lending strength, and
offering kind words like the wings of a bird.

so, though goodbyes may bring forth tears,
remember the shared laughter, the moments held
dear. for an airport gate is more than a physical space,
it's a reminder of our boundless embrace.

and as i take flight to lands yet unexplored,
i carry with me the memories, the love, forever
stored.

an ode to happy pills

in the quiet of my mind,
a storm once raged,
demons danced,
my world they crazed.

but happy, happy pills,
you came to my aid,
cleansed the chaos,
the fear you forbade.

with you,
i soar on clouds so high,
the weight of worry,
you bid goodbye.

hope blooms anew,
my heart's revival,
with each dose,
you mend my survival.

magic in a capsule,
a spark so bright,
guiding me through
the darkest night.

happy, happy pills,
my trusted friend,
you bring peace,
and for that,
i'll bend.

bend in gratitude,
for you've set me free,
from the chains of despair,
you've rescued me.

happy, happy pills,
a beacon in my strife,
thank you for restoring my life.

my mother's love

let me tell you something noteworthy
about my mother's love.

it's a mighty tree with branches stretched out,
arms open wide; tailor-made for a warm embrace—
i feel safe and loved. and upon that,
there are golden ornaments embellished in style,
brightly lit like a guiding light, guiding me home.

firmly rooted deep under the ground,
it flourishes and shoots up tall as a house,
though oftentimes seen as a skyscraper.

fine like an 'ace of hearts' redbud
with pink flowers on top,
she sees me right with great tenderness
and abiding love to the point
that nothing can be compared—
impeccable, to put it concretely.
the kind of love she has towards me is resilient—
a fortresslike tree that withstands gale-force winds
and raging storms: an enduring aegis.

embers of hope

there's gotta be more to life—
even if you haven't seen or found it yet,
even if it'll take you months or years
or even a decade to witness a breakthrough,
even if a state of emptiness feels like violent
jabs that only you could fathom,
even if downright silence sounds
like a head-splitting commotion
that only you could hear,
even if the clock is alarmingly ticking
like a ticking bomb, even if time passes by
so quickly that you've lost track of time
and forget what century you are in,
even if you feel like you can't endure
such pain any longer;
but here you are,
still breathing,
still standing on
your own two feet,
fighting against the odds.

know that you possess such dauntless bravery
and i'm immensely proud of you; **keep on staying
afloat, for my heart is truly gratified.**

night's melancholy

in the dead of night, you linger still,
haunting dreams with your ghostly chill,
awakening me from slumber deep,
in a cold sweat, i lie in a heap.

your memory, a cruel crime,
unpunished by the hands of time,
i surrendered, i gave in, to the heart
you sought, to win.

we both knew the end was nigh,
yet my heart refuses to comply,
beating wildly, against the odds,
clinging to hope, disregarding the gods.

isn't it tragic, isn't it sad, how we both lost
what we had, my home, now a broken shell,
waiting for your return, but all is farewell.

so here i wait, in the dead of night,
for dreams to fade, for dawn's first light,
hoping against hope, for a love that's flown,
knowing deep down, i'm alone.

if i could be a cat

if i could be a cat just for one day,
i would lay wherever life takes me.
i would be pleased to know that
i have nine lives to maneuver my ways
into opportunities without fearing risks.

i would believe in love at first pat,
knowing good hoomans do exist
as they come with gentle hands;
this is why i'd like to pick my owner,
this is why i would walk up to you
and insist on following you when you catch me
wandering around scattered garbage,
hunting for leftovers to satisfy my belly temporarily,
or just to fight for survival.

please know, i would be scared to
come near you at first, though—
still and all, kindly feed me as you're pleased
and show me that true love does exist.

it's okay if you can't take me in;
you have your reasons, and i totally understand.
but...it would be nice if you could.
i promise you that i would be your best ally

and snuggle with you when you seem out of place,
needing some company: i would be your best
cheerleader.

i wouldn't bother you if needs not be,
but...i would lay close to you or nap around you
to remind you of my presence just in case
you feel lonely, and i hope that's okay with you.

november (i)

crisp winds,
warm thick blankets,
windows open,
a new day is here—
when the air is a bit cooler
with drops of moisture touching
everything that lives and breathes.

i could feel the touch of cool
yet tender morning breeze,

brushing against my skin:
quite chilly but snuggly to tell of.

a cup of hot coffee placed on a bureau
by my window-pane keeps me sane;
aspired, all there in my right mind.

with leaves falling to the ground
and patchy drizzles rapping my tin roof,
november signals a time for reflection:
my life events, stories, and lessons
to be cherished and shared.

time ages like fine wine.
it fires me with enthusiasm,
my wildest imaginations of what could be,
for there is magnification in maturity,
thriving with endless possibilities.

one can easily get lost in thought,
drowning in a sea of hope; however,
the odds may be infinite yet untold—
you stay afloat when you keep your hope intact,
especially in tough times.

november (ii)

november happens when the presence
of chilly winds is apparent at times,
and warm, sunny days are springing back into
life with clear blue skies.

some like to be wrapped in their blankets,
getting cozy in their pajamas and feeling whole.
some may like to read or journal in the shade
where rays of light pass through a canopy
and birds chirp freely.

whereas some, in their fine array,
immerse themselves in cafes,
sipping their favorite hot latte
and enjoying their day
as if it were their last.

november is a reminder
that we're one step closer
to another year or, strangely enough,
another chapter of life—
we'll never know, won't we?
anything can happen in a span of time
and there are things in life we can't control;
however, we can always choose to look back
and reflect on them.

therein lies november, a force to be reckoned with.
it's when realization presents itself with mindfulness
and firmness of purpose: do better next time,
hopefully—and you will, with grace.

december

'tis the time of the year
when it truly feels magical
as the jolly season begins
with the arrival of the winter solstice.

all we see are those adorned lights
placed upon mistletoes,
window panes, or somewhere along sidewalks—
a timely reminder that **wherever we go, the light
follows.**

playing in the background is the sound of christmas
music, blasting out on repeat with contentment,
leaving nothing but melodic echos to fill the cold air
of nonchalance;
ergo, 'tis the season to sparkle and have a ball.

cozy sweaters have never felt
warmer for this nippy weather—
like one fine shelter to cover
and induce a warm embrace.

one can only imagine how lovely
it would be to sit under the mistletoe,
watching the snow falling while reminiscing
about those good old times.

on the night of the 24th,
when christmas is most roistered,
we can see lavish meals readily made
and laid upon spaciously long tables
just to satisfy appetite—enwreathed with
candle lights and christmas lights,
flickering and dazzling in the room.

december, that merry time of the year
that creates a homely atmosphere
filled with long talks, warm hugs,
laughter, tears, and gifts that are shared
and felt through the night—
oh, december, what a roller coaster ride
of memories untucked and reveled.

the way i'll miss you

i know perfectly well
that this all dominoes,
but i think i'm going to miss
the way you laugh so loud,
it entertains the crowds,
echoing like joy on a summer breeze,
lifting my spirit, a moment seized.

i think i'm going to miss the way
you hold your favorite reusable cup
that carries your favorite coffee
like a cherished ritual—
each sip a story,
each brew a chapter,
a comfort in the chaos,
your own little rapture.

i'm going to miss the way
you watch your favorite video game
that engulfs you in-between breaks,
a world you escape, pixels and dreams,
your eyes ablaze, lost in the magic,
the thrill, the chase.

i'm going to miss the way
you catch me looking at you shyly at times,

a glance, a spark, a silent rhyme,
my heart exposed, my feelings clear,
in those fleeting moments, you were near.

i know perfectly well
that nothing can be reciprocated,
but i'm glad that our paths have crossed
and you've made my heart smile again,
like a long-lost friend, a gift unexpected,
a connection untamed, in the puzzle of life,
a piece reclaimed.

31

turned 31 with aching bones, keeping me awake at
night with such pain i have begun to understand,
spiraling down my spine and keeping my
mindfulness at bay.

i have never felt more fragile than how i did 10 years
back. *it's a fact that the older you get, the more
fragile you are.* fine wrinkles are starting to take
shape like layers of life experienced with waves of
emotions bottled up.

a mind as sharp as a steel trap is slowly ebbing away
while prodigious memory containing all those stories
and events is noticeably fading to black. gray hair is
coming into view as a reminder that my time on earth
is finite and my existence with every little thing
that i can do to contribute to even just a single soul
will hopefully be considered as a remembrance.

that, regardless of how, does not mean turning 31
is one scary ride or a cry for help. i was taught that
everything has pros and cons and there are two sides
to every coin—'tis the liberty i hold dear to my heart.

i've learned that people may come and go as they're
pleased, but the show must always go on with, or
without 'em.
the beauty of my maturity is blossoming into a
garden of red roses with branches of love and
acceptance.

i have a loving family that loves me for who i am and
is always there for me. true friends who always have
my back and vouch for my journey in life. colleagues
who radiate positive energy by listening, guiding, and
understanding. favorite books and music to
accompany me while in isolation; dreams and goals
to cherish; places to explore and experiences to be
unraveled.

*so, dear life, thank you for being
such a rollercoaster ride.*

an electric touch

it had been ages since i felt
that electric spark,
a touch charged with magic.

let me linger in this dream,
believing you must have felt it, too.
i adored your sunny smile,
glowing under the moonlight,
with a hint of blush.

did you see how i trembled in my seat?
quivering is an indication of elation,
though sometimes, it means something else.

call me foolish, or lost in a dream,
but i can't let this beautiful moment
slip away so easily.

it had been a long time since i felt
that kind of touch, an electric touch.
let me wallow in this sheer fantasy,
assuming you must have felt it, too.

i loved how you wore your sunny expression
when you saw me. it shimmered in the moonlight
with a dash of blush.
*did you notice the way i was shaking
like a leaf in my seat?* quivering is an indication
of elation, although sometimes, it's not the case.

call me silly, or illusory, but i can't seem to let this
marvelous moment slip my mind that easily.

el nido

el nido, an island distant and secluded,
abounds with treasures and resources
beneath the sea, its waters appearing
a mesmerizing emerald blue,
a hue i never imagined could exist.

on a balmy summer morning,
the air is cool, carrying the blessing
of the salty sea—one can easily lose oneself
in such rare natural beauty.

crossing the philippine sea on a ferry,
sailing the vast pacific ocean,
i gaze upon marine life thriving
beneath crystal-clear waters,
a riot of colors reminiscent of rainbows.

submerging into the ocean's expanse,
i feel the gentle embrace of seawater,
its calmness akin to warm comfort,
truly embodying the magnificence
of palawan: the promised land.

a place of enchantment,
tempting a return,
a desire to stay,

to settle in
its captivating allure.

a decade wrapped

stepped into 2020
with a determined grip
on the will to live, learn,
and cherish. any chance,
albeit a small one,
is after all the drive to fuel
and fulfill my passion
with such dedication.

a decade flew by at the speed of light—
i have lost and found parts of myself stumbling
into and out of darkness, darting across fire and
flames.

i watched myself burn and crumble to dust,
leaving nothing but remaining fiery flickers
that have never faltered since.

i looked for a miraculous sign in the wrong places,
fell for the wrong people, and dived into a world
unknown.

i mistook lust for love. i rushed headlong into
romances one after another, just to escape the state of
loneliness
that i had forgotten what it meant to love myself

and feel whole. above all, i have learned, and i have
found the magic in me.

i now know that scars are beautiful landmarks
that have embarked on my journey and turning points
in life. i am surrounded by the right people.

i have friends and family who know me best,
and i no longer dress to impress. i have made peace
with my past and let things go with no judgment.

i am living my best life, and i look forward to
having it all together in another decade.

hope

78

hope is a double-edged sword—
a source of comfort,
or a cause of torment
when you cling to it.

we see hope as a flash of light
that glides through our
deep dark fears;
but hope is also a rope
with a hint of menace
that drives a nail into
the coffin of credence.

as a foil to one's austerity,
hope is to be kept alive
to some extent—
for expectations can be
the seeds of destruction.

september

now and then,
september has been the month
of reminiscence—a flash of remembrance
between my stagnation and transformation.

in the cool breeze, echoes of old days dance,
memories unfurl like the leaves of autumn,
drifting between what was and what's yet to be,
caught in the amber glow of september's dusk.

my obsession with change has never faltered,
albeit knowing that everything comes with a price,
especially if the change itself is in full blossom:
aspirations.

i've paid in moments, in heartbeats,
in fragments of my soul, each dream
a tender seed planted in fertile hopes,
growing, twisting, reaching for the skies,
yet roots anchored in the soil
of who i once was.

as september draws near,
making a dignified exit,
i light up each time
with sheer delight.

it's a dance of cycles,
endings and beginnings intertwined,
september, a bridge between past and future,
where i find myself in the in-between,
embracing the beauty of change,
the inevitability of growth,
and the joy of becoming.

infinite wonder

as i look at the sky, one might think
i'm ferreting around the moon,
searching for faint stars; rather strangely,
i'm seeing the sky shining
brightly in the pitch-dark night.

is the size of the earth really finite as quantified
by scientists? they map its curves, measure its girth,
yet miss the infinite stretch of wonder in my eyes.

curiosity kills the cat, but, truly, it's a sight to behold.
it sparks within me a relentless quest to uncover
the mysteries beyond the known, to wander where
light dares not roam, to find beauty

in the absence of certainty.
in the darkness, i see not just stars but dreams,
possibilities, the uncharted realms of thought.
each twinkle a whisper, a silent promise of
something more, something unseen,
waiting to be discovered.

so i gaze, not just with eyes but with soul,
embracing the unknown, cherishing the shadows,
for in the pitch-dark night, the sky shines brightly,
revealing the vastness of what we cannot yet
comprehend.

rachel

dear rachel,
you may not realize
that your name sounds like an angel,
but it does, apparently, as both words end in 'e.l.',
contriving a twin flame spell called rachangel;
this is why you are quite a charm.

dear rachel,
you exude an aura of beauty
that seemingly appears like a rose
immersed with the scent of its petals,
radiating from within that enthralls
everything all around; this is why
you are beautiful just like a rose.

dear rachel,
i thank you for being a rebel
in whatever you excel.
your sense of fashion propels
such convictions, statements,
and aspirations; and your confidence
shines like a brightly lit star
without a shadow of a doubt,
even in the dark;
darling, this is why you are a star.

dear rachel,
every time you dance,
you dance with joy;
and every time you move,
you move with grace—
i am truly amazed
because there is always a look
of ecstasy on your face;
this is why you dance like no other.
you light up everywhere you go,
and you should know how rare that is:
your impeccably dazzling soul.
thank you for being angelic.
thank you for being vocal.
but, most importantly,
thank you for being you.

the magic of taking a shower

do you know there's a touch of pure magic in taking a shower?

it doesn't matter how long it takes for you to get it done—even 2 minutes is worth the frailty. if the thought of it makes you sick and you get cold feet, please know that i, too, have been a victim of this nerve-wracking encounter on most days, aware of how drenched i'd get, and the way water drips, sliding down my back, putting me on edge.

but then i realized that my mind could trick me into such angst, which isn't always the fact of the matter.

and i believe that fear holds us back, relentlessly keeping us from knowing something inside out, relinquishing shadows haunted by past memories.

in a way, it's like a trajectory put in place for a flight-or-flight response. but rest assured, it can be conquered when your courage comes into the picture, plays its role, and defeats the beast that hides under the bed.

i used to stand there, paralyzed, the thought of water a waterfall of anxiety, imagining the cold shiver before the warmth could embrace me. each drop felt like a burden, a reminder of my vulnerability, the sound of water, a taunting whisper echoing my insecurities.

but i've learned that in the cascade there's a cleansing, a washing away of fears, a baptism of bravery, renewal in the simple act of being drenched, exposed, and alive.

it's in these moments, when i face the shower's downpour, that i find strength in surrender, courage in the currents, letting go of the weight that clings to my skin, allowing the flow to carry my doubts away.

and as the water cascades, i stand, a warrior in the stream, embracing the chill, the thrill, the undeniable magic in every drop, every breath, every heartbeat that reminds me *i am here, i am alive, and i can conquer anything.*

a touch of twilight

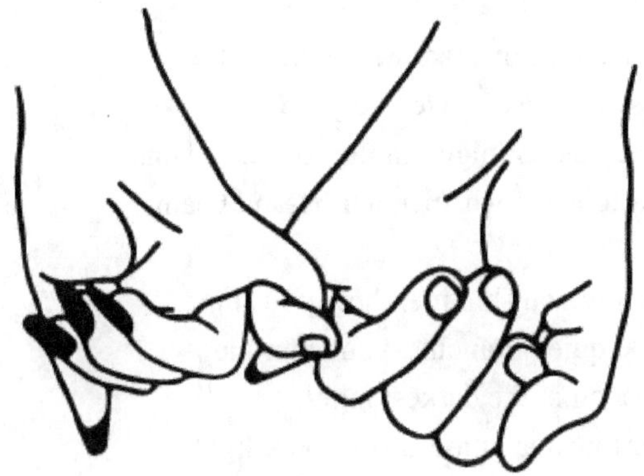

the way you touch my hand
sends a wave of jimjams,
making my heart crammed
with euphoria and bliss;

ah...the deft touch thou art endowed with,
drawing me in—making me itch for more;
like the flicker of candlelight,
burnin' so bright throughout the night;

oh, my goodness gracious!
thou art so full of life—mighty as a firefly,
glowin' and twinklin' in a nightlight
under the moonlit sky; right by your side.

your touch, a spark, a gentle nudge,
igniting flames that refuse to budge,

i feel the warmth, a tender glow,
in your presence, i find my flow.

like a dance of shadows on the wall,
we sway, we dip, we rise, we fall,
in the hush of night, in the still of dreams,
your touch, a whisper, a thousand beams.

oh, how you shimmer, how you shine,
in the quiet moments, you are mine,
a beacon in the darkest night,
your touch, a guide, a soft, pure light.

i marvel at the way you move,
effortless, with nothing to prove,
each touch, a story, each glance, a song,
in your embrace, where i belong.

so here we stand, hand in hand,
underneath the stars so grand,
with every touch, my heart takes flight,
dancing with you in the soft moonlight.

oh, my goodness gracious, how you amaze,
in your love, i find my gaze,
like a firefly, you light my way,
glowing, twinkling, night and day.

together, we shine, a radiant glow,
in your touch, my love does grow,

forever and always, side by side,
in this journey, our hearts abide.

the pursuit of happiness

the pursuit of happiness
shan't hinge on one's success;
but, rather, how content one is
with chips and splits of their quirkiness.

it's not about the trophies, the gold, the fame,
but the joy found in every little game,
in the quirks and the oddities we embrace,
in the laughter that lights up every face.

the pursuit of happiness
shall rest upon the belief that
life isn't about pleasing everyone,
and one must dare to dream and swing.

to dance to the beat of your own heart's song,
to stand tall in a world that says you're wrong,
to dream big, to swing high, to never relent,
for it's in those moments, true joy is spent.

in pursuit of happiness,
surround thyself with the kind of people—
dazzled by the beauty of life,
igniting your psyche and fanaticism.

find those who see the magic in the mundane,
who find joy in the sunshine and in the rain,
who light up your soul, who fan your flames,
who play with you in life's wondrous games.

the pursuit of happiness, a journey so grand,
not marked by the accolades or the stand,
but by the moments of pure, unfiltered glee,
in the company of those who let you be.

so seek not the applause, the world's empty praise,
but the smiles, the laughter, the sunny days,
for happiness dwells in the hearts that are free,
in the love, the dreams, the true you and me.

the precipice within

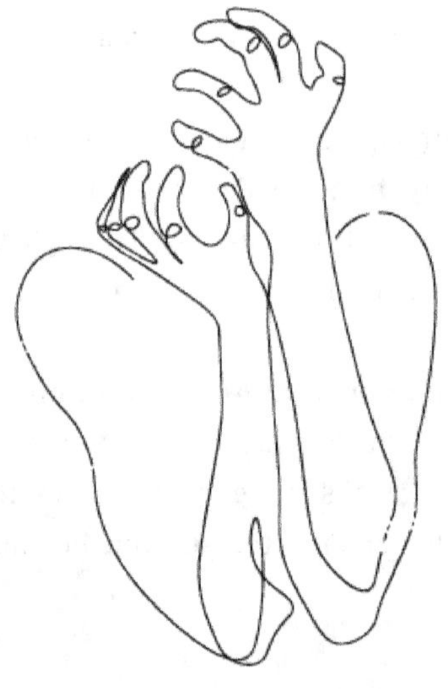

here i am,
standing on the brink of a cliff,
gasping for air,
screaming in silence;

with an unstable state of mind,
i find my hollows inside
striving to be free from this nullity
like a caged bird in captivity;

the depths of the sea might be
as deep as the ocean,

as high as the sky,
though i might go off the end
to vent my spleen on demise;

with every breath, a whisper of despair,
standing here, the weight's too much to bear,
the edge calls out, a siren's sweet song,
in this silence, i've been lost for too long;

the mind's a storm, a tempest raging wild,
i feel the echoes of a lost, lonely child,
yearning for freedom, for a release,
a break from this pain, a moment of peace;

like a bird trapped within these iron bars,
i dream of open skies, of distant stars,
to soar high above, to feel the wind's kiss,
to break these chains, to find what i've missed;

the sea below, a mirror of my soul,
reflecting the depths, the pieces not whole,
the sky above, an endless expanse,
a promise of escape, a second chance;

though i stand on this precipice, unsure,
the pull of the abyss, so tempting, so pure,
i must find the strength to step back, to fight,
to seek out the dawn, to embrace the light;

for in this struggle, i find my true call,
to rise above the void, to stand tall,
to mend the fractures, to heal the scars,
to find my freedom, to reach for the stars.

here i am,
on the brink, but not lost,
gasping for air,
but ready to exhaust;

with an unstable state of mind,
i seek the strength to leave behind
the shadows of despair, to truly be free,
like a bird released, soaring to infinity.

oh to be loved by a writer

oh, to be loved by a writer!
i could never imagine how lovely
it would be, but i'm entirely sure
that i would wake up each morning
to find sticky notes filled with honeyed phrases
or cute poems pinned against a fridge door
or maybe our hackneyed wall of memories
spent together. perhaps i would never get tired of it,
and you might catch me grinning like a cheshire cat,
knowing that the feeling is mutual.

i bet we would discuss a wide variety of books
we've read and poems that explode stars
in the galaxies or space or even mars
(i know i'm not an astronaut and i have no clue about
what i'm talking about, so i'll just paint all these
ideas in my head).

but one thing i do know is that the expansion of love
would stretch wide enough for you to try and try.
we would never run out of things to discuss.
he would lie on our favorite couch reading,
absorbed in his treasured newspapers or favorite
books, while i'm writing poems inspired by him and
the world around me.

he would be unable to take his eyes off me,
i'm sure of it, because he's already fallen deeply
in love with a poet who has caught his heart by
surprise.

a collection of sweet little things

- there's always something benevolent and benign in my neighborhood. a daughter in her 50s helps her mother in her 90s walk by placing her hand on her mother's waist like a side hug, letting her mother's whole body lean on hers for support. sometimes, our hands, arms, and hugs are better, and obviously warmer, than walking canes or any other tools available for those in need of help.

- a couple sits on a chaise lounge in a starbucks, enjoying each other's company in silence while working on their tasks. the woman, around 70, with her back against the couch, watches something beguiling on her mini smartphone, lost in her world with such curiosity. the man, around 60, likely her partner, types on his laptop, sorting through his piles of work. maybe this is what love looks like—not something as enchanting as what's unveiled in books or movies.

- the sun is up again after cloudy days and rainy nights. this is another reminder from the universe that whatever happened yesterday is over and no longer in our good graces. no matter the depth, let that be best remembered as a blessing in disguise, as in, better things are coming.

- a boy next door, about 5, whoops with laughter and excitement as his entire family sings a happy birthday song. their full-throated singing echoes through their home, concocting a sonorous yet lively tune that bursts through every crack of my windows, even though they were tightly shut. i feel a vicarious thrill of such delight and elation, knowing how a birthday treat can make a kid leap for joy.

- what a beautiful morning, watching a lady in her 20s make freshly homemade coffee for me in bliss. there was no indication of how its taste should be catered for, nor details needed. the way she poured out the milk into a crystal glass just to let it bask in the glory of richly warm coffee was an idyllic scene to behold.

- last saturday night, on a ride back home at 4 am, a dear friend of mine held my hand and

gently reminded me of how doughty i was to
have triumphed over the blues and the
dumps, and how blissed she was to see me
in high spirits again. prior to that, we had
danced wildly for joy, club hopping until the
night bit the dust and our knees trembled.
maybe this was a gesture of deep friendship
that we had cemented with nothing but pure,
abiding love. we've always been there for
each other, through quietude or
reconnecting. each honeyed moment is a
moment to be dwelled upon, held dear, and
known by heart.

- a girl, about 7, daughter of the owner of a
  japanese restaurant i often dine at, attempts
  to capture photographs of everything that
  tickles her fancy using a smartphone. i'm
  caught off guard when she takes a little peep
  at me, savoring my food. at that instant, she
  asks me to pose with my two fingers up like
  a symbol of peace and smile. i do as told,
  and a sudden gleam comes into her eyes and
  she is all smiles. small moments like this
  genuinely fondle my heart.

- finally understanding the nuances behind the
  'baby shark' song. my neighbor next door,
  staying in the same building on the 2nd
  floor, was teaching and singing the song to

her students, about 7 years old. this song usually drives most adults, myself included, up the wall. but it didn't get on my nerves this time. instead, my heart filled with elation, hearing her hearty little voice echoing through the silent premises, followed by the kids' sweet, sing-song voices resonating in the background, trying to pronounce each word correctly while singing along and keeping pace with the "doo doo doo doo doo" beats on repeat. the song now feels like a parade of unity and family to me, and i'm tickled pink whenever i hear it.

- there's this lovely puppy, my neighbor's, that always greets me by the door every morning. her face appears from her pet flap, curiously calm but with a rush of excitement—i can tell by the sound of her stomping feet, scurrying to meet and greet, each time my front door creaks when i open it.

- on the way home, a tuktuk driver in his 40s received a phone call from his dearest daughter, asking if he's already on his way home, as she tries to keep her hunger pangs at bay while waiting for his return to have dinner with her. he says, *i'm still*

working—please eat first—don't wait for me.
but she refuses, saying with deep emotion,
no, mum and i will wait for you to come
home first, papa. he is taken by surprise,
trying to keep his composure, yet there is a
hint of emotion in his eyes. right before she
hangs up, she says, take care, papa—be safe
on the way home. i, too, am left with such
tenderness upon overhearing it. sometimes,
a loved one's voice can cut through the
silence and paint the town red.

acknowledgments

gratitude to me has always been a bridge over
troubled water, shaping me into a better writer, poet,
and most importantly, a wholesome human.

with that in mind, i always start my thank-yous at the
beginning. i owe a significant debt to the person who
first brought me into contact with this divine world
called "poetry"—kyle, i wouldn't be here without
you. thank you for being an amazing friend,
ex-colleague, and ex-housemate. there's no doubt in
my mind that you're also a fine writer and poet.

to such distinguished and aspiring poets as emily
dickinson, jane austen, margaret atwood, taylor swift,
and sarah kay, i cannot thank you enough for being
the backbone of my imaginative and creative writing.
your books, poems, and music have eminently honed
my writing skills to date.

to alma, rachel, and tinzi, thank you for always being
great and sympathetic listeners. it may sound cheesy,
but you are the first people i want to share my work
with each time i write a new poem. no words can
express how grateful i am. *thank you for being more
than friends. thank you for showing up with avidity.*

to sochie, thank you for your vivid and striking
illustrations illuminating my poems.

finally, a dedication. if this book is a success, i would
like to dedicate it to my exes, the places i've been,
midnight hours, and both happy and troubled times
that i dived into and survived. this book wouldn't be
possible without them.

and last but not least, **i thank you—my readers.**
thank you for purchasing this book. i hope you'll
enjoy reading and feast your eyes on your favorite
pieces. please let me know if you do!

about the author

mckenzie vlad, a writer and poet hailing from cambodia, was born in 1992. his life is a tapestry woven with words, music, and stories. by day, he works as a copywriter and translator, but his heart beats strongest when he is crafting poetry, immersing himself in melodies, or diving into the pages of a book.

his poetic journey began in 2018, a year that marked a profound transformation. seeking solace from his pain, he found an unexpected healer in poetry. at first, his verses were mere fragments—one or two lines capturing fleeting emotions. yet, with relentless dedication, he nurtured his craft, eventually composing full-length and spoken-word poems.

to mckenzie, poetry is a divine gift, a precious offering from the universe. he trusts in the power of his words to touch hearts and heal souls, transcending physical boundaries. his verses delve into themes of love, heartbreak, human experiences, places, and the intricate tapestry of feelings. through his art, he invites readers to embark on journeys to deep, dark, or beautifully illuminated places that inspire his poetry.

when he isn't weaving words into verses, mckenzie
enjoys the simple pleasures of life—cafe hopping and
engaging in deep, meaningful conversations, even
with strangers. his curiosity and openness enrich his
experiences and fuel his creativity. holding a
bachelor's degree in education, mckenzie has always
felt a magnetic pull towards literature and writing.

his passion for the written word was ignited in 2015
when he began his career as a content producer. from
that moment, he has been unwavering in his
commitment to his craft, continually evolving as a
storyteller and poet.

about the illustrator

sochie is renowned as a masterful digital and visual storyteller, enchanting audiences in cambodia with his art, drawings, sketches, and paintings. his unparalleled ability to breathe life into characters from scratch—whether inspired by anime, movies, or tv series—sets him apart in the artistic realm. sochie's talent has graced various pop-up events across cambodia, where his graphic arts captivate and inspire. in his free time, he luxuriates in the comfort of his bed, immersing himself in the enchanting worlds of gaming.

currently, he weaves his creative magic as a digital artist for a private advertising agency, dedicating each day to honing his craft. to witness the vivid tapestry of sochiet's work, visit some of his best work at https://linktr.ee/sochie.arts and experience the enchanting worlds he brings to life.